THIS JOURNAL BELONGS TO

....

TO LOVE ONESELF IS THE
BEGINNING
OF A LIFELONG
ROMANCE.
~Oscar Wilde~

by THE GENTLE NOTEBOOK

the gentle notebook

WANT A FREEBIE !?

Follow us on Instagram
@gentlenotebook

&

Email us at
thegentlenotebook@gmail.com

Title your email with our secret code "U808", let us know that you have followed us and we will send some extra SURPRISES your way!

We create our journals with love and great care.

Yet mistakes can always happen. For any issues with your journal, such as faulty binding, printing errors, or something else, please do not hesitate to contact us by sending us a DM/Inbox at Instagram @gentlenotebook

We will make sure you get a replacement copy immediately.

DESIGNED by The Gentle Notebook

Unstoppable - Food & Fitness Journal
Copyright © The Gentle Notebook 2020 - All rights reserved.

Hey! You are Awesome

Glue in a photo of yourself, not the perfect one! So you can look back at it at the end of your journey and be amazed!

DARLING YOU ARE A GODDESS AND ONCE YOU KNOW WHAT THAT TRULY MEANS YOU BECOME

✨ UNSTOPPABLE ✨

What made you decide to start this journey?

....
....
....

How would you rate your self-esteem and confidence today on a scale of 1-10?

1   2   3   4   5   6   7   8   9   10

Don't Break Your Heart
Progress Tracker

Color Your Day

RED
If Completed

Yellow
If Completed partially
(e.g. missed out fitness log, water intake etc.)

Black
If Skipped

My Measurements: Let's Get Started

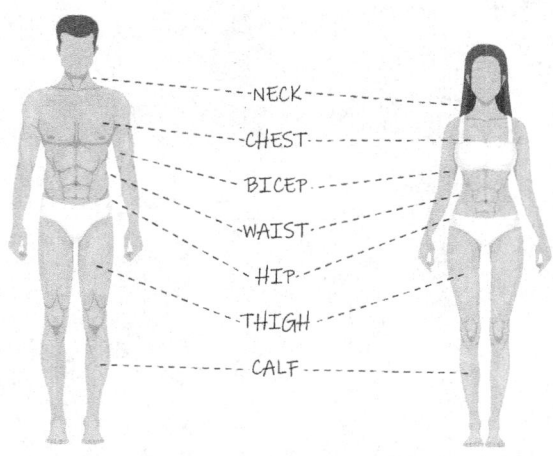

.... NECK

.... CHEST

.... BICEP

.... WAIST

.... HIP

.... THIGH

.... CALF

.... HEIGHT

.... WEIGHT

.... OTHERS

Measurement Progress

	WEEK 1	WEEK 2	WEEK 3	WEEK 4	WEEK 5	WEEK 7	WEEK 9	Final Week 11
NECK								
CHEST								
BICEPS								
WAIST								
HIPS								
THIGHS								
CALVES								
HEIGHT								
WEIGHT								
BMI								

Goal

_____
_____

Why do you want to achieve this goal?

_____
_____
_____

~ My Milestones ~

Day 30

_____

Day 60

_____

Day 80

_____

What are the first 3 things you will do to kick-start your goal?

1. _____
2. _____
3. _____

2
Goal

_____
_____

Why do you want to achieve this goal?

_____
_____
_____

~ My Milestones ~

Day 30
_____

Day 60
_____

Day 80
_____

What are the first 3 things you will do to kick-start your goal?

1. _____
   _____

2. _____
   _____

3. _____
   _____

Goal

_____
_____

Why do you want to achieve this goal?

_____
_____
_____

~ My Milestones ~

Day 30

_____

Day 60

_____

Day 80

_____

What are the first 3 things you will do to kick-start your goal?

1. _____
   _____

2. _____
   _____

3. _____
   _____

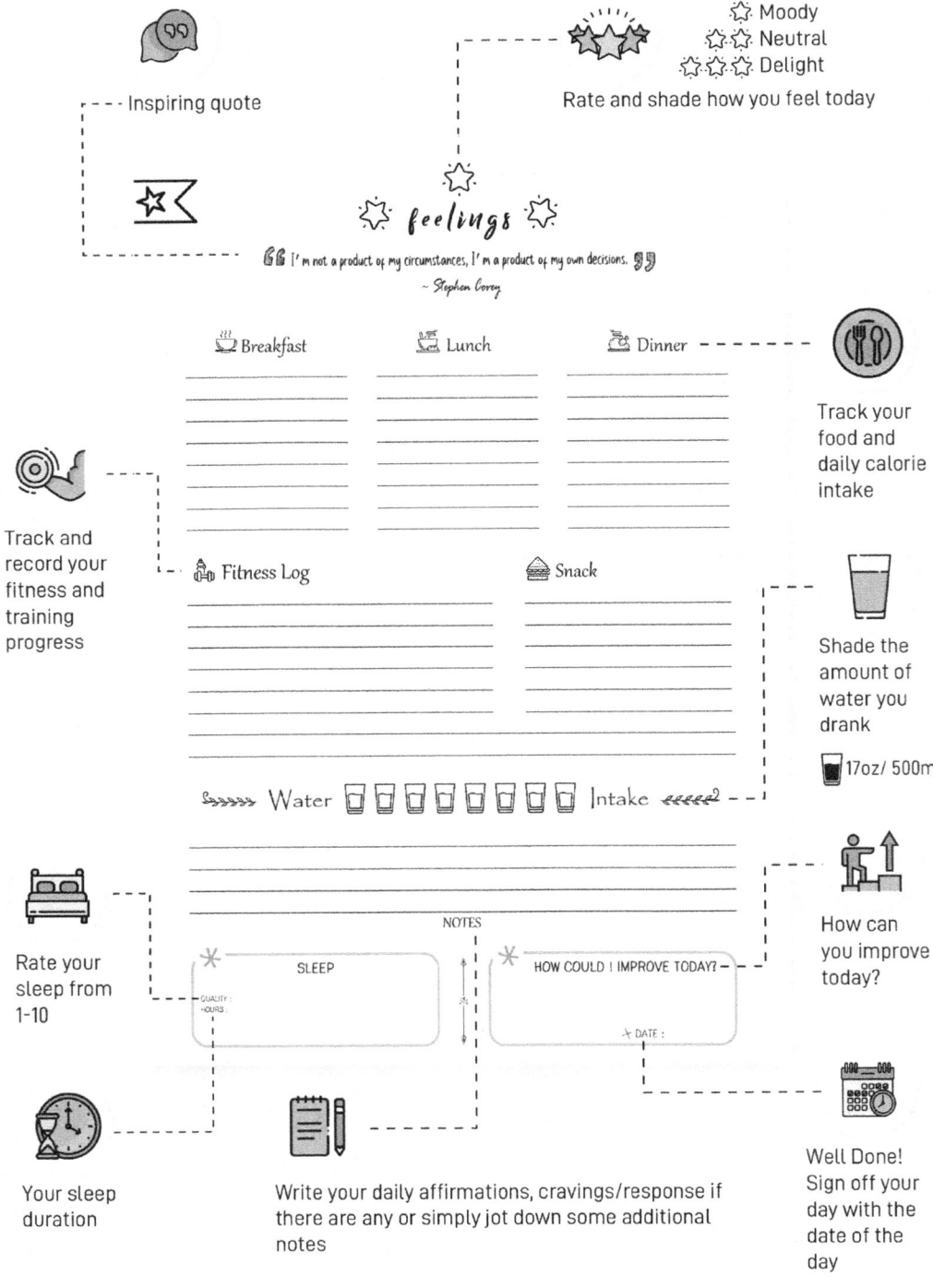

feelings

> "A dream becomes a goal when action is taken toward its achievement."
> ~ Bo Bennett

☕ Breakfast

_____
_____
_____
_____
_____
_____
_____

🍲 Lunch

_____
_____
_____
_____
_____
_____
_____

🍗 Dinner

_____
_____
_____
_____
_____
_____
_____

🏋 Fitness Log

_____
_____
_____
_____
_____
_____
_____

🥪 Snack

_____
_____
_____
_____
_____
_____
_____

Water 🥛🥛🥛🥛🥛🥛🥛 Intake

_____
_____
_____

NOTES

SLEEP
QUALITY :
HOURS :

HOW COULD I IMPROVE TODAY?

✕ DATE :

> It's what you practice in private that you will be rewarded for in public.
> ~ Tony Robbins

☕ Breakfast

_____
_____
_____
_____
_____
_____
_____

🥘 Lunch

_____
_____
_____
_____
_____
_____
_____

🍲 Dinner

_____
_____
_____
_____
_____
_____
_____

🏋 Fitness Log

_____
_____
_____
_____
_____
_____
_____

🥪 Snack

_____
_____
_____
_____
_____
_____
_____

Water 🥛🥛🥛🥛🥛🥛🥛 Intake

_____
_____
_____

NOTES

SLEEP
QUALITY :
HOURS :

HOW COULD I IMPROVE TODAY?

DATE :

> I don't focus on what I'm up against. I focus on my goals and I try to ignore the rest.
> ~ Venus Williams

☕ Breakfast
_____
_____
_____
_____
_____
_____
_____
_____

🥣 Lunch
_____
_____
_____
_____
_____
_____
_____
_____

🍗 Dinner
_____
_____
_____
_____
_____
_____
_____
_____

🏋️ Fitness Log
_____
_____
_____
_____
_____
_____
_____

🥪 Snack
_____
_____
_____
_____
_____
_____
_____

Water 🥛🥛🥛🥛🥛🥛🥛 Intake

_____
_____
_____

NOTES

SLEEP
QUALITY :
HOURS :

HOW COULD I IMPROVE TODAY?

DATE :

feelings

> *Successful people keep moving. They make mistakes, but they don't quit.*
> ~ Conrad Hilton

Breakfast
_____
_____
_____
_____
_____
_____
_____

Lunch
_____
_____
_____
_____
_____
_____
_____

Dinner
_____
_____
_____
_____
_____
_____
_____

Fitness Log
_____
_____
_____
_____
_____
_____
_____

Snack
_____
_____
_____
_____
_____
_____

Water ☐ ☐ ☐ ☐ ☐ ☐ ☐ Intake

NOTES
_____
_____
_____

SLEEP
QUALITY :
HOURS :

HOW COULD I IMPROVE TODAY?

DATE :

feelings

> "Action is the foundational key to all success."
> ~ Pablo Picasso

☕ Breakfast
_____
_____
_____
_____
_____
_____
_____

🍽 Lunch
_____
_____
_____
_____
_____
_____
_____

🍗 Dinner
_____
_____
_____
_____
_____
_____
_____

🏋 Fitness Log
_____
_____
_____
_____
_____
_____
_____
_____

🥪 Snack
_____
_____
_____
_____
_____
_____
_____
_____

~~~~~ Water 🥛🥛🥛🥛🥛🥛🥛🥛 Intake ~~~~~

_____
_____
_____

NOTES

SLEEP
QUALITY :
HOURS :

HOW COULD I IMPROVE TODAY?

DATE :

☆ feelings ☆

> "Everyone who got where he is has had to begin where he was."
> ~ Robert Louis Stevenson

☕ Breakfast
_____
_____
_____
_____
_____
_____
_____

🍽 Lunch
_____
_____
_____
_____
_____
_____
_____

🍗 Dinner
_____
_____
_____
_____
_____
_____
_____

🏋 Fitness Log
_____
_____
_____
_____
_____
_____
_____

🥪 Snack
_____
_____
_____
_____
_____
_____
_____

Water 🥛🥛🥛🥛🥛🥛🥛 Intake

_____
_____
_____

NOTES

SLEEP
QUALITY :
HOURS :

HOW COULD I IMPROVE TODAY?

✶ DATE :

☆ feelings ☆

> Be miserable. Or motivate yourself. Whatever has to be done, it's always your choice.
> ~ Wayne Dyer

☕ Breakfast

_____
_____
_____
_____
_____
_____
_____

🍲 Lunch

_____
_____
_____
_____
_____
_____
_____

🍗 Dinner

_____
_____
_____
_____
_____
_____
_____

🏋 Fitness Log

_____
_____
_____
_____
_____
_____

🥪 Snack

_____
_____
_____
_____
_____
_____

~~~ Water 🥛 🥛 🥛 🥛 🥛 🥛 🥛 Intake ~~~

_____
_____
_____

NOTES

SLEEP
QUALITY :
HOURS :

HOW COULD I IMPROVE TODAY?

DATE :

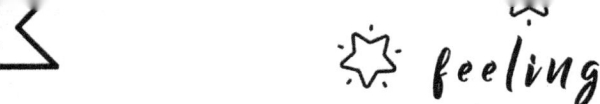

> It's perseverance that's the key. It's persevering for long enough to achieve your potential.
> ~ Lynn Davies

☕ Breakfast

_____
_____
_____
_____
_____
_____
_____
_____

🍜 Lunch

_____
_____
_____
_____
_____
_____
_____
_____

🍗 Dinner

_____
_____
_____
_____
_____
_____
_____
_____

🏋 Fitness Log

_____
_____
_____
_____
_____
_____
_____
_____
_____

🥪 Snack

_____
_____
_____
_____
_____
_____
_____

Water 🥛🥛🥛🥛🥛🥛🥛 Intake

_____
_____
_____

NOTES

SLEEP
QUALITY :
HOURS :

HOW COULD I IMPROVE TODAY?

✕ DATE :

"The man who never makes mistakes is the man who never does anhything."
~ Theodore Roosevelt

Breakfast

_____
_____
_____
_____
_____
_____
_____

Lunch

_____
_____
_____
_____
_____
_____
_____

Dinner

_____
_____
_____
_____
_____
_____
_____

Fitness Log

_____
_____
_____
_____
_____
_____
_____

Snack

_____
_____
_____
_____
_____
_____

Water Intake

_____
_____
_____

NOTES

SLEEP
QUALITY :
HOURS :

HOW COULD I IMPROVE TODAY?

DATE :

> Nothing great ever came that easy.
> ~ Kresley Cole

☕ Breakfast
_____
_____
_____
_____
_____
_____
_____

🍲 Lunch
_____
_____
_____
_____
_____
_____
_____

🍗 Dinner
_____
_____
_____
_____
_____
_____
_____

🏋 Fitness Log
_____
_____
_____
_____
_____
_____
_____

🥪 Snack
_____
_____
_____
_____
_____
_____
_____

Water 🥛🥛🥛🥛🥛🥛🥛🥛 Intake

_____
_____

NOTES

SLEEP	HOW COULD I IMPROVE TODAY?
QUALITY :	
HOURS :	DATE :

feelings

> 'Good, better, best. Never let it rest.' Til your good is better and your better is best.
> ~ St. Jerome

☕ Breakfast

_____
_____
_____
_____
_____
_____
_____

🍜 Lunch

_____
_____
_____
_____
_____
_____
_____

🍗 Dinner

_____
_____
_____
_____
_____
_____
_____

🏋 Fitness Log

_____
_____
_____
_____
_____
_____

🥪 Snack

_____
_____
_____
_____
_____
_____

Water 🥛🥛🥛🥛🥛🥛🥛 Intake

_____
_____

NOTES

SLEEP
QUALITY :
HOURS :

HOW COULD I IMPROVE TODAY?

DATE :

I never dreamed about success. I worked for it.
~ Estee Lauder

☕ Breakfast

🍲 Lunch

🦃 Dinner

🏋 Fitness Log

🥪 Snack

Water Intake

NOTES

SLEEP
QUALITY :
HOURS :

HOW COULD I IMPROVE TODAY?

DATE :

✦ feelings ✦

> *It is in your moments of decision that your destiny is shaped.*
> ~ Tony Robbins

☕ Breakfast

_____
_____
_____
_____
_____
_____

🍽 Lunch

_____
_____
_____
_____
_____
_____

🍗 Dinner

_____
_____
_____
_____
_____
_____

🏋 Fitness Log

_____
_____
_____
_____
_____
_____

🥪 Snack

_____
_____
_____
_____
_____

～ Water 🥛🥛🥛🥛🥛🥛🥛 Intake ～

_____
_____
_____
_____

NOTES

SLEEP
QUALITY :
HOURS :

HOW COULD I IMPROVE TODAY?

✕ DATE :

> When you reach the end of your rope, tie a knot in it and hang on.
> ~ Franklin D. Roosevelt

☕ Breakfast   🍜 Lunch   🍲 Dinner

🏋 Fitness Log   🥪 Snack

〜 Water 🥛🥛🥛🥛🥛🥛🥛 Intake 〜

NOTES

SLEEP
QUALITY :
HOURS :

HOW COULD I IMPROVE TODAY?

✛ DATE :

feelings

> "Optimism is the faith that leads to achievement. Nothing can without hope and confidence."
> ~ Helen Keller

☕ Breakfast
_____
_____
_____
_____
_____
_____
_____

🍲 Lunch
_____
_____
_____
_____
_____
_____
_____

🍗 Dinner
_____
_____
_____
_____
_____
_____
_____

🏋 Fitness Log
_____
_____
_____
_____
_____
_____
_____
_____

🥪 Snack
_____
_____
_____
_____
_____
_____
_____
_____

～ Water 🥛🥛🥛🥛🥛🥛🥛🥛 Intake ～

_____
_____
_____

NOTES

SLEEP
QUALITY :
HOURS :

HOW COULD I IMPROVE TODAY?

✕ DATE :

> To be successful, the first thing to do is fall in love with your work.
> ~ Sister Mary Lauretta

☕ Breakfast
_____
_____
_____
_____
_____
_____
_____

🍲 Lunch
_____
_____
_____
_____
_____
_____
_____

🍗 Dinner
_____
_____
_____
_____
_____
_____
_____

🏋 Fitness Log
_____
_____
_____
_____
_____

🥪 Snack
_____
_____
_____
_____
_____

Water 🥛🥛🥛🥛🥛🥛🥛🥛 Intake

_____
_____
_____

NOTES

SLEEP
QUALITY :
HOURS :

HOW COULD I IMPROVE TODAY?

DATE :

feelings

> *Only I can change my life. No one can do it for me.*
> ~ Carol Burnett

Breakfast

_____
_____
_____
_____
_____
_____
_____

Lunch

_____
_____
_____
_____
_____
_____
_____

Dinner

_____
_____
_____
_____
_____
_____
_____

Fitness Log

_____
_____
_____
_____
_____
_____

Snack

_____
_____
_____
_____
_____
_____

Water ☐ ☐ ☐ ☐ ☐ ☐ ☐ Intake

_____
_____
_____

NOTES

SLEEP
QUALITY :
HOURS :

HOW COULD I IMPROVE TODAY?

DATE :

> The road to success begins with knowing what you need to know and why.
> ~ Savania China

☕ Breakfast

_____
_____
_____
_____
_____
_____
_____

🍱 Lunch

_____
_____
_____
_____
_____
_____
_____

🍗 Dinner

_____
_____
_____
_____
_____
_____
_____

🏋 Fitness Log

_____
_____
_____
_____
_____
_____
_____
_____

🥪 Snack

_____
_____
_____
_____
_____
_____
_____
_____

Water ▯ ▯ ▯ ▯ ▯ ▯ ▯ ▯ Intake

_____
_____
_____

NOTES

SLEEP
QUALITY :
HOURS :

HOW COULD I IMPROVE TODAY?

DATE :

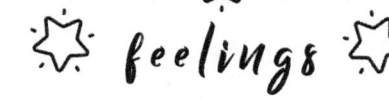

feelings

> *Even if you're on the right track, you'll get run over if you just sit there.*
> ~ Will Rogers

☕ **Breakfast**   🍱 **Lunch**   🍗 **Dinner**

_____   _____   _____
_____   _____   _____
_____   _____   _____
_____   _____   _____
_____   _____   _____
_____   _____   _____
_____   _____   _____

🏋 **Fitness Log**   🥪 **Snack**

_____   _____
_____   _____
_____   _____
_____   _____
_____   _____
_____   _____
_____   _____

~~~~~ **Water** 🥛 🥛 🥛 🥛 🥛 🥛 🥛 **Intake** ~~~~~

_____
_____
_____

NOTES

✶ **SLEEP**   ✶ **HOW COULD I IMPROVE TODAY?**

QUALITY :
HOURS :

                                                                    ✕ DATE :

feelings

> "The only thing that's keeping you from getting what you want is the story you keep telling yourself."
> ~ Tony Robbins

☕ Breakfast

_____
_____
_____
_____
_____
_____
_____
_____

🍽 Lunch

_____
_____
_____
_____
_____
_____
_____
_____

🍗 Dinner

_____
_____
_____
_____
_____
_____
_____
_____

🏋 Fitness Log

_____
_____
_____
_____
_____
_____
_____
_____

🥪 Snack

_____
_____
_____
_____
_____
_____
_____
_____

Water 🥛🥛🥛🥛🥛🥛🥛🥛 Intake

_____
_____
_____

NOTES

SLEEP
QUALITY :
HOURS :

HOW COULD I IMPROVE TODAY?

✛ DATE :

feelings

> "What the mind can conceive and believe, and the heart desire, you can achieve."
> ~ Norman Vincent Peale

☕ Breakfast
_____
_____
_____
_____
_____
_____
_____

🍲 Lunch
_____
_____
_____
_____
_____
_____
_____

🍗 Dinner
_____
_____
_____
_____
_____
_____
_____

🏋 Fitness Log
_____
_____
_____
_____
_____
_____
_____

🥪 Snack
_____
_____
_____
_____
_____
_____
_____

Water 🥛🥛🥛🥛🥛🥛🥛 Intake

_____
_____
_____

NOTES

SLEEP
QUALITY :
HOURS :

HOW COULD I IMPROVE TODAY?

✲ DATE :

… **feelings** …

> *We are what we repeatedly do. Excellence, then, is not an art, but a habit.*
> ~ Aristotle

☕ Breakfast
_____
_____
_____
_____
_____
_____
_____

🍜 Lunch
_____
_____
_____
_____
_____
_____
_____

🍗 Dinner
_____
_____
_____
_____
_____
_____
_____

🏋 Fitness Log
_____
_____
_____
_____
_____
_____

🥪 Snack
_____
_____
_____
_____
_____
_____

Water ▢ ▢ ▢ ▢ ▢ ▢ ▢ ▢ **Intake**

_____
_____

NOTES

SLEEP	HOW COULD I IMPROVE TODAY?
QUALITY :	
HOURS :	DATE :

… **feelings** …

> Go confidently in the direction of your dreams. Live the life you have imagined.
> ~ Henry David Thoreau

☕ Breakfast
_____
_____
_____
_____
_____
_____
_____

🍜 Lunch
_____
_____
_____
_____
_____
_____
_____

🍗 Dinner
_____
_____
_____
_____
_____
_____
_____

🏋️ Fitness Log
_____
_____
_____
_____
_____
_____

🥪 Snack
_____
_____
_____
_____
_____
_____

Water 🥛🥛🥛🥛🥛🥛🥛 Intake

NOTES
_____
_____
_____

SLEEP
QUALITY :
HOURS :

HOW COULD I IMPROVE TODAY?

✕ DATE :

✧ feelings ✧

> You don't have to be great to start, but you have to start to be great.
> ~ Zig Ziglar

☕ Breakfast

_____
_____
_____
_____
_____
_____
_____

🍲 Lunch

_____
_____
_____
_____
_____
_____
_____

🍗 Dinner

_____
_____
_____
_____
_____
_____
_____

🏋 Fitness Log

_____
_____
_____
_____
_____
_____
_____

🥪 Snack

_____
_____
_____
_____
_____
_____

～ Water 🥛🥛🥛🥛🥛🥛🥛 Intake ～

_____
_____
_____

NOTES

SLEEP
QUALITY :
HOURS :

HOW COULD I IMPROVE TODAY?

✕ DATE :

feelings

" There is nothing permanent except change. "
~ Heraclitus

☕ Breakfast　　　🍽 Lunch　　　🍗 Dinner

🏋 Fitness Log　　　🥪 Snack

Water 🥛🥛🥛🥛🥛🥛🥛 Intake

NOTES

SLEEP
QUALITY :
HOURS :

HOW COULD I IMPROVE TODAY?

✶ DATE :

feelings

> *Life begins at the end of your comfort zone.*
> ~ Neale Donald Walsh

☕ Breakfast
_____
_____
_____
_____
_____
_____
_____

🍜 Lunch
_____
_____
_____
_____
_____
_____
_____

🍲 Dinner
_____
_____
_____
_____
_____
_____
_____

🏋 Fitness Log
_____
_____
_____
_____
_____
_____
_____

🥪 Snack
_____
_____
_____
_____
_____
_____
_____

Water 🥛🥛🥛🥛🥛🥛 Intake

_____
_____
_____

NOTES

SLEEP
QUALITY :
HOURS :

HOW COULD I IMPROVE TODAY?

✲ DATE :

feelings

> Find a place inside where there's joy, and the joy will burn out the pain.
> ~ Joseph Campbell

☕ Breakfast

_____
_____
_____
_____
_____
_____
_____

🍲 Lunch

_____
_____
_____
_____
_____
_____
_____

🍗 Dinner

_____
_____
_____
_____
_____
_____
_____

🏋️ Fitness Log

_____
_____
_____
_____
_____
_____
_____

🥪 Snack

_____
_____
_____
_____
_____
_____
_____

~~~~~ Water 🥛 🥛 🥛 🥛 🥛 🥛 🥛 🥛 Intake ~~~~~

_____
_____
_____

NOTES

SLEEP
QUALITY :
HOURS :

HOW COULD I IMPROVE TODAY?

✕ DATE :

Things work out best for those who make the best of how things work out.
~ John Wooden

☕ Breakfast

🍲 Lunch

🍗 Dinner

🏋 Fitness Log

🥪 Snack

Water 🥛🥛🥛🥛🥛🥛🥛🥛 Intake

NOTES

SLEEP
QUALITY :
HOURS :

HOW COULD I IMPROVE TODAY?

DATE :

… feelings …

> "Don't judge each day by the harvest you reap but by the seeds that you plant."
> ~ Robert Louis Stevenson

Breakfast

_____
_____
_____
_____
_____
_____
_____

Lunch

_____
_____
_____
_____
_____
_____
_____

Dinner

_____
_____
_____
_____
_____
_____
_____

Fitness Log

_____
_____
_____
_____
_____
_____

Snack

_____
_____
_____
_____
_____
_____

Water 🥛🥛🥛🥛🥛🥛🥛🥛 Intake

_____
_____
_____

NOTES

SLEEP
QUALITY :
HOURS :

HOW COULD I IMPROVE TODAY?

DATE :

> *Perfection is not attainable, but if we chase perfection we can catch excellence.*
> ~ Vince Lombardi

☕ Breakfast
_____
_____
_____
_____
_____
_____
_____

🍽 Lunch
_____
_____
_____
_____
_____
_____
_____

🍗 Dinner
_____
_____
_____
_____
_____
_____
_____

🏋 Fitness Log
_____
_____
_____
_____
_____
_____
_____

🥪 Snack
_____
_____
_____
_____
_____
_____

Water 🥛🥛🥛🥛🥛🥛🥛 Intake

_____
_____

NOTES

SLEEP
QUALITY :
HOURS :

HOW COULD I IMPROVE TODAY?

DATE :

> The only thing necessary for the triumph of evil is for good men to do nothing.
> ~ Edmund Burke

☕ Breakfast

_____
_____
_____
_____
_____
_____
_____

🍲 Lunch

_____
_____
_____
_____
_____
_____
_____

🍗 Dinner

_____
_____
_____
_____
_____
_____
_____

🏋️ Fitness Log

_____
_____
_____
_____
_____
_____

🥪 Snack

_____
_____
_____
_____
_____
_____

Water 🥛🥛🥛🥛🥛🥛🥛 Intake

_____
_____
_____

NOTES

SLEEP
QUALITY :
HOURS :

HOW COULD I IMPROVE TODAY?

✕ DATE :

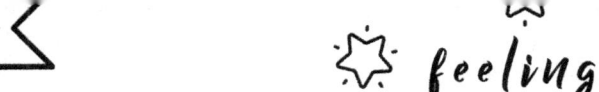

feelings

> "Life is 10% what happens to you and 90% how you react to it."
> ~ Charles R. Swindoll

☕ Breakfast
_____
_____
_____
_____
_____
_____

🍜 Lunch
_____
_____
_____
_____
_____
_____

🍲 Dinner
_____
_____
_____
_____
_____
_____

🏋️ Fitness Log
_____
_____
_____
_____
_____
_____
_____

🥪 Snack
_____
_____
_____
_____
_____
_____
_____

🌿 Water 🥛🥛🥛🥛🥛🥛🥛🥛 Intake 🌿

_____
_____
_____

NOTES

SLEEP
QUALITY :
HOURS :

HOW COULD I IMPROVE TODAY?

✦ DATE :

 feelings

> "Success is not final, failure is not fatal: it is the courage to continue that counts."
> ~ Winston Churchill

☕ Breakfast

_____
_____
_____
_____
_____
_____
_____

🍽 Lunch

_____
_____
_____
_____
_____
_____
_____

🍗 Dinner

_____
_____
_____
_____
_____
_____
_____

🏋 Fitness Log

_____
_____
_____
_____
_____
_____
_____
_____
_____

🥪 Snack

_____
_____
_____
_____
_____
_____
_____
_____
_____

～ Water 🥛🥛🥛🥛🥛🥛🥛 Intake ～

_____
_____
_____
_____

NOTES

SLEEP
QUALITY :
HOURS :

HOW COULD I IMPROVE TODAY?

✕ DATE :

☆ feelings ☆

> *It's not what we do once in a while that shapes our lives, but what we do consistently.*
> ~ Tony Robbins

☕ Breakfast

_____
_____
_____
_____
_____
_____
_____

🍲 Lunch

_____
_____
_____
_____
_____
_____
_____

🍗 Dinner

_____
_____
_____
_____
_____
_____
_____

🏋 Fitness Log

_____
_____
_____
_____
_____
_____

🥪 Snack

_____
_____
_____
_____
_____
_____

_____
_____

Water 🥛🥛🥛🥛🥛🥛🥛🥛 Intake

_____
_____
_____

NOTES

SLEEP
QUALITY :
HOURS :

HOW COULD I IMPROVE TODAY?

✦ DATE :

feelings

> *Our greatest glory is not in never falling, but in rising every time we fall.*
> ~ Confucius

☕ Breakfast

_____
_____
_____
_____
_____
_____
_____

🍜 Lunch

_____
_____
_____
_____
_____
_____
_____

🍗 Dinner

_____
_____
_____
_____
_____
_____
_____

🏋️ Fitness Log

_____
_____
_____
_____
_____
_____
_____

🥪 Snack

_____
_____
_____
_____
_____
_____
_____

Water 🥛 🥛 🥛 🥛 🥛 🥛 🥛 Intake

_____
_____
_____

NOTES

SLEEP
QUALITY :
HOURS :

HOW COULD I IMPROVE TODAY?

✕ DATE :

> *Do not go where the path may lead, go instead where there is no path and leave a trail.*
> ~ Ralph Waldo Emerson

☕ Breakfast

_____
_____
_____
_____
_____
_____
_____

🍽 Lunch

_____
_____
_____
_____
_____
_____
_____

🍗 Dinner

_____
_____
_____
_____
_____
_____
_____

🏋 Fitness Log

_____
_____
_____
_____
_____
_____
_____
_____

🥪 Snack

_____
_____
_____
_____
_____
_____

Water 🥛🥛🥛🥛🥛🥛🥛 Intake

_____
_____
_____

NOTES

SLEEP
QUALITY :
HOURS :

HOW COULD I IMPROVE TODAY?

DATE :

feelings

> "In three words I can sum up everything I've learned about life: it goes on."
> ~ Robert Frost

☕ Breakfast

_____
_____
_____
_____
_____
_____
_____

🍱 Lunch

_____
_____
_____
_____
_____
_____
_____

🍗 Dinner

_____
_____
_____
_____
_____
_____
_____

🏋️ Fitness Log

_____
_____
_____
_____
_____
_____
_____

🥪 Snack

_____
_____
_____
_____
_____
_____

🌿 Water 🥛🥛🥛🥛🥛🥛🥛 Intake 🌿

_____
_____
_____

NOTES

✶ SLEEP
QUALITY :
HOURS :

✶ HOW COULD I IMPROVE TODAY?

✶ DATE :

> *Don't wish it were easier. Wish you were better.*
> ~ Jim Rohn

☕ Breakfast
_____
_____
_____
_____
_____
_____
_____

🍜 Lunch
_____
_____
_____
_____
_____
_____
_____

🍗 Dinner
_____
_____
_____
_____
_____
_____
_____

🏋️ Fitness Log
_____
_____
_____
_____
_____
_____

🍔 Snack
_____
_____
_____
_____
_____
_____

Water 🥛 🥛 🥛 🥛 🥛 🥛 🥛 Intake

_____
_____
_____

NOTES

SLEEP
QUALITY :
HOURS :

HOW COULD I IMPROVE TODAY?

DATE :

feelings

"Change your thoughts and you change your world."
~ Norman Vincent Peale

Breakfast

_____
_____
_____
_____
_____
_____
_____

Lunch

_____
_____
_____
_____
_____
_____
_____

Dinner

_____
_____
_____
_____
_____
_____
_____

Fitness Log

_____
_____
_____
_____
_____
_____
_____
_____

Snack

_____
_____
_____
_____
_____
_____
_____
_____

Water Intake

_____
_____
_____

NOTES

SLEEP
QUALITY :
HOURS :

HOW COULD I IMPROVE TODAY?
DATE :

feelings

> *Everything you've ever wanted is on the other side of fear.*
> ~ George Addair

☕ Breakfast

_____
_____
_____
_____
_____
_____
_____

🍲 Lunch

_____
_____
_____
_____
_____
_____
_____

🍗 Dinner

_____
_____
_____
_____
_____
_____
_____

🏋 Fitness Log

_____
_____
_____
_____
_____
_____

🥪 Snack

_____
_____
_____
_____
_____
_____

Water ▯▯▯▯▯▯▯▯ Intake

_____
_____
_____

NOTES

SLEEP
QUALITY :
HOURS :

HOW COULD I IMPROVE TODAY?

DATE :

feelings

> "The starting point of all achievement is desire."
> ~ Napoleon Hill

☕ Breakfast
_____
_____
_____
_____
_____
_____
_____

🍽 Lunch
_____
_____
_____
_____
_____
_____
_____

🍗 Dinner
_____
_____
_____
_____
_____
_____
_____

🏋 Fitness Log
_____
_____
_____
_____
_____
_____
_____

🥪 Snack
_____
_____
_____
_____
_____
_____

Water 🥛🥛🥛🥛🥛🥛🥛 Intake

_____
_____
_____

NOTES

SLEEP
QUALITY :
HOURS :

HOW COULD I IMPROVE TODAY?

✝ DATE :

feelings

> *I will not let anyone walk through my mind with their dirty feet.*
> ~ Mahatma Ghandi

☕ **Breakfast**   🍜 **Lunch**   🍗 **Dinner**

_____

🏋️ **Fitness Log**   🍔 **Snack**

_____

🌿 **Water** 🥛🥛🥛🥛🥛🥛🥛 **Intake** 🌿

_____

NOTES

✱ **SLEEP**
QUALITY :
HOURS :

✱ **HOW COULD I IMPROVE TODAY?**

✚ DATE :

> The only person you are destined to become is the person you decide to be.
> ~ Ralph Waldo Emerson

☕ Breakfast
_____
_____
_____
_____
_____
_____
_____

🍜 Lunch
_____
_____
_____
_____
_____
_____
_____

🍗 Dinner
_____
_____
_____
_____
_____
_____
_____

🏋 Fitness Log
_____
_____
_____
_____
_____
_____

🥪 Snack
_____
_____
_____
_____
_____
_____

~~~~~ Water 🥛🥛🥛🥛🥛🥛🥛 Intake ~~~~~

_____
_____
_____

NOTES

✱ SLEEP	✱ HOW COULD I IMPROVE TODAY?
QUALITY :	
HOURS :	✚ DATE :

> There is only one thing that makes a dream impossible to achieve: the fear of failure.
> ~ Paulo Coelho

☕ Breakfast

_____
_____
_____
_____
_____
_____
_____
_____

🍲 Lunch

_____
_____
_____
_____
_____
_____
_____
_____

🍗 Dinner

_____
_____
_____
_____
_____
_____
_____
_____

🏋 Fitness Log

_____
_____
_____
_____
_____
_____
_____
_____

🥪 Snack

_____
_____
_____
_____
_____
_____
_____

～ Water 🥛🥛🥛🥛🥛🥛🥛🥛 Intake ～

_____
_____
_____

NOTES

SLEEP
QUALITY :
HOURS :

HOW COULD I IMPROVE TODAY?

✢ DATE :

☆ feelings ☆

> "It's not whether you get knocked down. It's whether you get up."
> ~ Vince Lombardi

☕ Breakfast
_____
_____
_____
_____
_____
_____
_____
_____

🍜 Lunch
_____
_____
_____
_____
_____
_____
_____
_____

🍗 Dinner
_____
_____
_____
_____
_____
_____
_____
_____

🏋️ Fitness Log
_____
_____
_____
_____
_____
_____

🍔 Snack
_____
_____
_____
_____
_____
_____

ᔕᔕᔕ Water 🥛🥛🥛🥛🥛🥛🥛🥛 Intake ᔕᔕᔕ

_____
_____
_____

NOTES

SLEEP
QUALITY :
HOURS :

HOW COULD I IMPROVE TODAY?

✕ DATE :

feelings

"Opportunities don't happen, you create them."
~ Chris Grosser

Breakfast

Lunch

Dinner

Fitness Log

Snack

Water Intake

NOTES

SLEEP
QUALITY :
HOURS :

HOW COULD I IMPROVE TODAY?

DATE :

☆ feelings ☆

> *Work harder on yourself than you do on your job.*
> ~ Jim Rohn

☕ Breakfast

🥣 Lunch

🍗 Dinner

🏋 Fitness Log

🥪 Snack

〰 Water 🥛🥛🥛🥛🥛🥛🥛🥛 Intake 〰

NOTES

✻ SLEEP
QUALITY :
HOURS :

✻ HOW COULD I IMPROVE TODAY?

✕ DATE :

feelings

> *Definiteness of purpose is the starting point of all achievement.*
> ~ W. Clement Stone

☕ Breakfast
_____
_____
_____
_____
_____
_____
_____

🍱 Lunch
_____
_____
_____
_____
_____
_____
_____

🍗 Dinner
_____
_____
_____
_____
_____
_____
_____

🏋 Fitness Log
_____
_____
_____
_____
_____
_____
_____

🥪 Snack
_____
_____
_____
_____
_____
_____

Water 🥛🥛🥛🥛🥛🥛🥛 Intake

_____
_____

NOTES

SLEEP
QUALITY :
HOURS :

HOW COULD I IMPROVE TODAY?

✕ DATE :

feelings

> *All generalizations are false, including this one.*
> ~ Mark Twain

☕ Breakfast

_____
_____
_____
_____
_____
_____
_____

🍽 Lunch

_____
_____
_____
_____
_____
_____
_____

🍗 Dinner

_____
_____
_____
_____
_____
_____
_____

🏋 Fitness Log

_____
_____
_____
_____
_____
_____
_____
_____

🥪 Snack

_____
_____
_____
_____
_____
_____

Water 🥛🥛🥛🥛🥛🥛🥛 Intake

_____
_____
_____

NOTES

SLEEP
QUALITY :
HOURS :

HOW COULD I IMPROVE TODAY?

✦ DATE :

> Too many of us are not living our dreams because we are living our fears.
> ~ Les Brown

☕ Breakfast

_____
_____
_____
_____
_____
_____

🍜 Lunch

_____
_____
_____
_____
_____
_____

🍲 Dinner

_____
_____
_____
_____
_____
_____

🏋️ Fitness Log

_____
_____
_____
_____
_____
_____

🥪 Snack

_____
_____
_____
_____
_____
_____

Water 🥛🥛🥛🥛🥛🥛🥛 Intake

_____
_____
_____

NOTES

SLEEP
QUALITY :
HOURS :

HOW COULD I IMPROVE TODAY?

✕ DATE :

☆ feelings ☆

> *What you become is far more important than what you get.*
> ~ Jim Rohn

☕ Breakfast

_____
_____
_____
_____
_____
_____
_____
_____

🍜 Lunch

_____
_____
_____
_____
_____
_____
_____
_____

🍗 Dinner

_____
_____
_____
_____
_____
_____
_____
_____

🏋️ Fitness Log

_____
_____
_____
_____
_____
_____
_____

🥪 Snack

_____
_____
_____
_____
_____
_____
_____

Water 🥛 🥛 🥛 🥛 🥛 🥛 🥛 🥛 Intake

_____
_____
_____

NOTES

SLEEP
QUALITY :
HOURS :

HOW COULD I IMPROVE TODAY?

DATE :

> **Strength does not come from physical capacity. It comes from an indomitable will.**
> ~ Mahatma Gandhi

☕ Breakfast
_____
_____
_____
_____
_____
_____
_____

🍲 Lunch
_____
_____
_____
_____
_____
_____
_____

🍲 Dinner
_____
_____
_____
_____
_____
_____
_____

🏋 Fitness Log
_____
_____
_____
_____
_____
_____

🍔 Snack
_____
_____
_____
_____
_____

〜 Water 🥛🥛🥛🥛🥛🥛🥛🥛 Intake 〜

_____
_____
_____

NOTES

✴ **SLEEP**
QUALITY :
HOURS :

✴ **HOW COULD I IMPROVE TODAY?**

✛ DATE :

feelings

> "Life does not get better by chance, it gets better by change."
> ~ Jim Rohn

☕ Breakfast

_____
_____
_____
_____
_____
_____
_____

🍜 Lunch

_____
_____
_____
_____
_____
_____
_____

🍗 Dinner

_____
_____
_____
_____
_____
_____
_____

🏋️ Fitness Log

_____
_____
_____
_____
_____
_____
_____
_____

🥪 Snack

_____
_____
_____
_____
_____
_____
_____
_____

~~~~~ Water 🥛🥛🥛🥛🥛🥛🥛🥛 Intake ~~~~~

_____
_____
_____

NOTES

✳ SLEEP
QUALITY :
HOURS :

✳ HOW COULD I IMPROVE TODAY?

✕ DATE :

The greatest pleasure in life is doing what people say you cannot do.
~ Walter Bagehot

☕ Breakfast
_____
_____
_____
_____
_____
_____
_____

🍽 Lunch
_____
_____
_____
_____
_____
_____
_____

🍗 Dinner
_____
_____
_____
_____
_____
_____
_____

🏋 Fitness Log
_____
_____
_____
_____
_____
_____
_____

🥪 Snack
_____
_____
_____
_____
_____
_____
_____

Water 🥛🥛🥛🥛🥛🥛🥛 Intake

_____
_____

NOTES

SLEEP
QUALITY :
HOURS :

HOW COULD I IMPROVE TODAY?

DATE :

> *The most difficult thing is the decision to act, the rest is merely tenacity.*
> ~ Amelia Earhart

☕ Breakfast   🍲 Lunch   🍗 Dinner

🏋 Fitness Log   🥪 Snack

〰 Water 🥛🥛🥛🥛🥛🥛🥛 Intake 〰

NOTES

SLEEP
QUALITY :
HOURS :

HOW COULD I IMPROVE TODAY?

✦ DATE :

feelings

> The best revenge is massive success.
> ~ walt Sinatra

☕ Breakfast

🍜 Lunch

🍗 Dinner

🏋 Fitness Log

🥪 Snack

Water 🥛🥛🥛🥛🥛🥛🥛 Intake

NOTES

SLEEP
QUALITY :
HOURS :

HOW COULD I IMPROVE TODAY?

✳ DATE :

feelings

> You can never cross the ocean until you have the courage to lose sight of the shore.
> ~ Christopher Columbus

☕ Breakfast
_____
_____
_____
_____
_____
_____
_____
_____

🍱 Lunch
_____
_____
_____
_____
_____
_____
_____
_____

🍗 Dinner
_____
_____
_____
_____
_____
_____
_____
_____

🏋 Fitness Log
_____
_____
_____
_____
_____
_____
_____

🥪 Snack
_____
_____
_____
_____
_____
_____
_____

Water 🥛🥛🥛🥛🥛🥛🥛 Intake

_____
_____
_____

NOTES

SLEEP
QUALITY :
HOURS :

HOW COULD I IMPROVE TODAY?

DATE :

✧ feelings ✧

> If you talk about it, it's a dream, if you envision it, it's possible, but if you schedule it, it's real.
> ~ Tony Robbins

☕ Breakfast

_____
_____
_____
_____
_____
_____
_____

🍱 Lunch

_____
_____
_____
_____
_____
_____
_____

🍗 Dinner

_____
_____
_____
_____
_____
_____
_____

🏋 Fitness Log

_____
_____
_____
_____
_____
_____
_____

🥪 Snack

_____
_____
_____
_____
_____
_____
_____

∽∽∽ Water 🥛🥛🥛🥛🥛🥛🥛 Intake ∽∽∽

_____
_____
_____

NOTES

SLEEP
QUALITY :
HOURS :

HOW COULD I IMPROVE TODAY?

✕ DATE :

feelings

> "The future belongs to those who believe in the beauty of their dreams."
> ~ Franklin D. Roosevelt

☕ Breakfast

_____
_____
_____
_____
_____
_____
_____

🍲 Lunch

_____
_____
_____
_____
_____
_____
_____

🍗 Dinner

_____
_____
_____
_____
_____
_____
_____

🏋 Fitness Log

_____
_____
_____
_____
_____
_____
_____

🥪 Snack

_____
_____
_____
_____
_____
_____

ᔆᔆᔆ Water 🥛🥛🥛🥛🥛🥛🥛 Intake ᔆᔆᔆ

_____
_____
_____

NOTES

SLEEP
QUALITY :
HOURS :

HOW COULD I IMPROVE TODAY?

✕ DATE :

feelings

> *In order to carry a positive action we must develop here a positive vision.*
> ~ Dalai Lama

☕ **Breakfast**

🍲 **Lunch**

🍗 **Dinner**

🏋 **Fitness Log**

🥪 **Snack**

Water 🥛🥛🥛🥛🥛🥛🥛 **Intake**

NOTES

SLEEP
QUALITY :
HOURS :

HOW COULD I IMPROVE TODAY?

✶ DATE :

❝ Don't be pushed around by the fears in your mind. Be led by the dreams in your heart. ❞
~ Roy T. Bennett

☕ Breakfast

_____
_____
_____
_____
_____
_____
_____

🥣 Lunch

_____
_____
_____
_____
_____
_____
_____

🍗 Dinner

_____
_____
_____
_____
_____
_____
_____

🏋 Fitness Log

_____
_____
_____
_____
_____
_____
_____

🥪 Snack

_____
_____
_____
_____
_____
_____
_____

～ Water 🥛🥛🥛🥛🥛🥛🥛 Intake ～

_____
_____
_____

NOTES

SLEEP
QUALITY :
HOURS :

HOW COULD I IMPROVE TODAY?

✚ DATE :

feelings

> *It does not matter how slowly you go as long as you do not stop.*
> ~ Confucius

☕ Breakfast
_____
_____
_____
_____
_____
_____
_____

🍱 Lunch
_____
_____
_____
_____
_____
_____
_____

🍗 Dinner
_____
_____
_____
_____
_____
_____
_____

🏋 Fitness Log
_____
_____
_____
_____
_____
_____

🥪 Snack
_____
_____
_____
_____
_____
_____

Water Intake 🥛🥛🥛🥛🥛🥛🥛🥛

NOTES
_____
_____
_____

SLEEP
QUALITY :
HOURS :

HOW COULD I IMPROVE TODAY?

DATE :

 feelings

> "Ever tried. Ever failed. No matter. Try again. Fail again. Fail better."
> ~ Samuel Beckett

☕ Breakfast
_____
_____
_____
_____
_____
_____
_____

🍲 Lunch
_____
_____
_____
_____
_____
_____
_____

🍛 Dinner
_____
_____
_____
_____
_____
_____
_____

🏋️ Fitness Log
_____
_____
_____
_____
_____
_____

🥪 Snack
_____
_____
_____
_____
_____
_____

Water 🥛🥛🥛🥛🥛🥛🥛 Intake

_____
_____
_____

NOTES

SLEEP
QUALITY :
HOURS :

HOW COULD I IMPROVE TODAY?

✱ DATE :

☆ feelings ☆

" Whatever the mind can conceive and believe, it can achieve. "
~ Napoleon Hill

☕ Breakfast
___
___
___
___
___
___
___

🍲 Lunch
___
___
___
___
___
___
___

🍗 Dinner
___
___
___
___
___
___
___

🏋 Fitness Log
___
___
___
___
___
___

🍔 Snack
___
___
___
___
___
___

Water 🥛🥛🥛🥛🥛🥛🥛🥛 Intake

___
___
___

NOTES

SLEEP
QUALITY :
HOURS :

HOW COULD I IMPROVE TODAY?

✕ DATE :

feelings

> *The odds of hitting your target go up dramatically when you aim at it.*
> ~ Mal Pancoast

Breakfast

_____
_____
_____
_____
_____
_____
_____

Lunch

_____
_____
_____
_____
_____
_____
_____

Dinner

_____
_____
_____
_____
_____
_____
_____

Fitness Log

_____
_____
_____
_____
_____
_____
_____

Snack

_____
_____
_____
_____
_____
_____
_____

Water ☐ ☐ ☐ ☐ ☐ ☐ ☐ ☐ Intake

_____
_____
_____

NOTES

SLEEP
QUALITY :
HOURS :

HOW COULD I IMPROVE TODAY?

DATE :

> *Fortune always favors the brave, and never helps a man who does not help himself.*
> ~ P. T. Barnum

☕ Breakfast

_____
_____
_____
_____
_____
_____
_____
_____

🍱 Lunch

_____
_____
_____
_____
_____
_____
_____
_____

🍗 Dinner

_____
_____
_____
_____
_____
_____
_____
_____

🏋 Fitness Log

_____
_____
_____
_____
_____
_____
_____

🥪 Snack

_____
_____
_____
_____
_____
_____
_____

Water 🥛🥛🥛🥛🥛🥛🥛 Intake

NOTES

_____
_____
_____

SLEEP
QUALITY :
HOURS :

HOW COULD I IMPROVE TODAY?

✦ DATE :

> Some people say you're going the wrong way, when it's simply a way of your own.
> ~ Angelina Jolie

☕ Breakfast

_____
_____
_____
_____
_____
_____
_____
_____

🍽 Lunch

_____
_____
_____
_____
_____
_____
_____
_____

🍗 Dinner

_____
_____
_____
_____
_____
_____
_____
_____

🏋 Fitness Log

_____
_____
_____
_____
_____
_____
_____
_____
_____

🥪 Snack

_____
_____
_____
_____
_____
_____
_____
_____
_____

Water 🥛🥛🥛🥛🥛🥛🥛 Intake

_____
_____
_____

NOTES

SLEEP
QUALITY :
HOURS :

HOW COULD I IMPROVE TODAY?

DATE :

 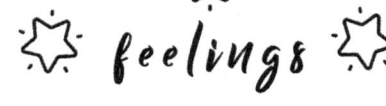

> It is during our darkest moments that we must focus to see the light.
> ~ Aristotle

☕ Breakfast
_____
_____
_____
_____
_____
_____
_____

🍽 Lunch
_____
_____
_____
_____
_____
_____
_____

🚴 Dinner
_____
_____
_____
_____
_____
_____
_____

🏋 Fitness Log
_____
_____
_____
_____
_____
_____

🥪 Snack
_____
_____
_____
_____
_____

~~~ Water 🥛🥛🥛🥛🥛🥛🥛 Intake ~~~

_____
_____
_____

NOTES

SLEEP
QUALITY :
HOURS :

HOW COULD I IMPROVE TODAY?

✕ DATE :

☆ feelings ☆

❝ If you look at what you have in life, you'll always have more. ❞
~ Oprah Winfrey

☕ Breakfast

_____
_____
_____
_____
_____
_____
_____

🍱 Lunch

_____
_____
_____
_____
_____
_____
_____

🍗 Dinner

_____
_____
_____
_____
_____
_____
_____

🏋 Fitness Log

_____
_____
_____
_____
_____
_____

🥪 Snack

_____
_____
_____
_____
_____
_____

～ Water 🥛🥛🥛🥛🥛🥛🥛 Intake ～

_____
_____
_____

NOTES

SLEEP
QUALITY :
HOURS :

HOW COULD I IMPROVE TODAY?

DATE :

> *A goal is not always meant to be reached, it often serves simply as something to aim at.*
> ~ Bruce Lee

☕ Breakfast
_____
_____
_____
_____
_____
_____
_____

🍜 Lunch
_____
_____
_____
_____
_____
_____
_____

🍲 Dinner
_____
_____
_____
_____
_____
_____
_____

🏋️ Fitness Log
_____
_____
_____
_____
_____
_____

🍔 Snack
_____
_____
_____
_____
_____
_____

Water 🥛🥛🥛🥛🥛🥛🥛 Intake

_____
_____
_____

NOTES

SLEEP
QUALITY :
HOURS :

HOW COULD I IMPROVE TODAY?

✕ DATE :

⭐ feelings ⭐

" Life shrinks or expands in proportion to one's courage. "
~ Anaïs Nin

☕ Breakfast

🍲 Lunch

🍛 Dinner

🏋 Fitness Log

🥪 Snack

Water 🥛🥛🥛🥛🥛🥛🥛 Intake

NOTES

SLEEP
QUALITY :
HOURS :

HOW COULD I IMPROVE TODAY?

DATE :

feelings

> It always seems impossible until it's done.
> ~ Nelson Mandela

☕ Breakfast
_____
_____
_____
_____
_____
_____
_____

🍱 Lunch
_____
_____
_____
_____
_____
_____
_____

🍗 Dinner
_____
_____
_____
_____
_____
_____
_____

🏋 Fitness Log
_____
_____
_____
_____
_____
_____
_____

🥪 Snack
_____
_____
_____
_____
_____
_____
_____

Water 🥛🥛🥛🥛🥛🥛🥛 Intake

_____
_____
_____

NOTES

SLEEP
QUALITY :
HOURS :

HOW COULD I IMPROVE TODAY?

✦ DATE :

> I'm not a product of my circumstances, I'm a product of my own decisions.
> ~ Stephen Covey

☕ Breakfast
_____
_____
_____
_____
_____
_____
_____

🥪 Lunch
_____
_____
_____
_____
_____
_____
_____

🍗 Dinner
_____
_____
_____
_____
_____
_____
_____

🏋 Fitness Log
_____
_____
_____
_____
_____
_____
_____

🥪 Snack
_____
_____
_____
_____
_____
_____
_____

Water 🥛🥛🥛🥛🥛🥛🥛🥛 Intake

_____
_____
_____

NOTES

SLEEP
QUALITY :
HOURS :

HOW COULD I IMPROVE TODAY?

✛ DATE :

feelings

> If you don't know where you are going, you'll end up someplace else.
> ~ Yogi Berra

☕ Breakfast
_____
_____
_____
_____
_____
_____
_____

🍜 Lunch
_____
_____
_____
_____
_____
_____
_____

🍗 Dinner
_____
_____
_____
_____
_____
_____
_____

🏋 Fitness Log
_____
_____
_____
_____
_____
_____
_____

🍔 Snack
_____
_____
_____
_____
_____
_____
_____

~~~~ Water 🥛🥛🥛🥛🥛🥛🥛🥛 Intake ~~~~

_____
_____
_____

NOTES

✳ SLEEP
QUALITY :
HOURS :

✳ HOW COULD I IMPROVE TODAY?

✦ DATE :

> When you want to succeed as bad as you want to breathe, then you'll be successful.
> ~ Eric Thomas

Breakfast

_____
_____
_____
_____
_____
_____

Lunch

_____
_____
_____
_____
_____
_____

Dinner

_____
_____
_____
_____
_____
_____

Fitness Log

_____
_____
_____
_____
_____
_____
_____

Snack

_____
_____
_____
_____
_____
_____
_____

Water ▯▯▯▯▯▯▯▯ Intake

_____
_____
_____

NOTES

SLEEP
QUALITY :
HOURS :

HOW COULD I IMPROVE TODAY?

DATE :

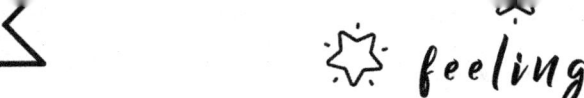

feelings

" Work like there is someone else working twenty-four hours a day to take it away from you. "
~ Mark Cuban

☕ Breakfast   🍲 Lunch   🍗 Dinner

🏋 Fitness Log   🥪 Snack

〰 Water 🥛🥛🥛🥛🥛🥛🥛🥛 Intake 〰

NOTES

SLEEP
QUALITY :
HOURS :

HOW COULD I IMPROVE TODAY?

✕ DATE :

☆ feelings ☆

> *Hard work beats talent when talent doesn't work hard.*
> ~ Tim Nothe

☕ Breakfast
_____
_____
_____
_____
_____
_____
_____
_____

🍲 Lunch
_____
_____
_____
_____
_____
_____
_____
_____

🍗 Dinner
_____
_____
_____
_____
_____
_____
_____
_____

🏋 Fitness Log
_____
_____
_____
_____
_____
_____
_____

🥪 Snack
_____
_____
_____
_____
_____
_____
_____

~ Water 🥛🥛🥛🥛🥛🥛🥛🥛 Intake ~

_____
_____
_____

NOTES

✻ SLEEP

QUALITY :
HOURS :

✻ HOW COULD I IMPROVE TODAY?

✛ DATE :

feelings

> "Failure is the opportunity to begin again more intelligently."
> ~ Henry Ford

☕ Breakfast

_____
_____
_____
_____
_____
_____
_____
_____

🍱 Lunch

_____
_____
_____
_____
_____
_____
_____
_____

🍲 Dinner

_____
_____
_____
_____
_____
_____
_____
_____

🏋 Fitness Log

_____
_____
_____
_____
_____
_____
_____
_____

🥪 Snack

_____
_____
_____
_____
_____
_____
_____
_____

~ Water 🥛🥛🥛🥛🥛🥛🥛🥛 Intake ~

_____
_____
_____

NOTES

✻ SLEEP
QUALITY :
HOURS :

✻ HOW COULD I IMPROVE TODAY?

✦ DATE :

> Learn how to be happy with what you have while pursue all that you want.
> ~ Jim Rohn

Breakfast

Lunch

Dinner

Fitness Log

Snack

Water Intake

NOTES

SLEEP
QUALITY :
HOURS :

HOW COULD I IMPROVE TODAY?

DATE :

feelings

> "A good goal is like a strenuous exercise – it makes you stretch."
> ~ Mary Kay Ash

☕ Breakfast

_____
_____
_____
_____
_____
_____
_____

🍜 Lunch

_____
_____
_____
_____
_____
_____
_____

🍲 Dinner

_____
_____
_____
_____
_____
_____
_____

🏋 Fitness Log

_____
_____
_____
_____
_____
_____

🍔 Snack

_____
_____
_____
_____
_____
_____

Water 🥛🥛🥛🥛🥛🥛🥛🥛 Intake

NOTES

_____
_____
_____

SLEEP
QUALITY :
HOURS :

HOW COULD I IMPROVE TODAY?

✝ DATE :

BE YOUR OWN HERO

My Results

Write down 3 things that you have achieved so far

1. _____

2. _____

3. _____

List 3 things that you have learned in the process

1. _____

2. _____

3. _____

Write down 3 things that you have failed

1. _____

2. _____

3. _____

Why have you failed?

1. _____

2. _____

3. _____

YOU HAVE COME A LONG WAY GIRL! WELL DONE! BE PROUD, BE CONFIDENT, & CELEBRATE!

My Fasting Log

Date: ....

Quality .... Sleep .... Hrs

12.00 AM	
1.00 AM	
2.00 AM	
3.00 AM	
4.00 AM	
5.00 AM	
6.00 AM	
7.00 AM	
8.00 AM	
9.00 AM	
10.00 AM	
11.00 AM	
12.00 PM	
1.00 PM	
2.00 PM	
3.00 PM	
4.00 PM	
5.00 PM	
6.00 PM	
7.00 PM	
8.00 PM	
9.00 PM	
10.00 PM	
11.00 PM	
12.00 AM	

Activity / Physical State

....
....
....
....
....

Mental & Emotional State

....
....
....
....
....

Water Intake
🥛 🥛 🥛 🥛 🥛 🥛 🥛

How could you improve today?
....
....

Daily affirmations, I am :
....
....
....

Weight : ....

Additional notes
....
....
....
....
....

Hours Fasted : ....

My Fasting Log

Date: ....

12.00 AM
1.00 AM
2.00 AM
3.00 AM
4.00 AM
5.00 AM
6.00 AM
7.00 AM
8.00 AM
9.00 AM
10.00 AM
11.00 AM
12.00 PM
1.00 PM
2.00 PM
3.00 PM
4.00 PM
5.00 PM
6.00 PM
7.00 PM
8.00 PM
9.00 PM
10.00 PM
11.00 PM
12.00 AM

Quality .... Sleep .... Hrs

....
....

Activity / Physical State

....
....
....
....
....
....

Mental & Emotional State

....
....
....
....
....
....

Water 🥛 🥛 🥛 🥛 🥛 🥛 🥛 Intake

How could you improve today?
....
....

Daily affirmations, I am :
....
....
....

Additional notes
....
....
....
....
....

Weight : ....   Hours Fasted : ....

My Fasting Log

Date:

12.00 AM
1.00 AM
2.00 AM
3.00 AM
4.00 AM
5.00 AM
6.00 AM
7.00 AM
8.00 AM
9.00 AM
10.00 AM
11.00 AM
12.00 PM
1.00 PM
2.00 PM
3.00 PM
4.00 PM
5.00 PM
6.00 PM
7.00 PM
8.00 PM
9.00 PM
10.00 PM
11.00 PM
12.00 AM

Quality .... Sleep .... Hrs

....
....

Activity / Physical State

....
....
....
....

Mental & Emotional State

....
....
....
....

Water ☐ ☐ ☐ ☐ ☐ ☐ ☐ ☐ Intake

How could you improve today?

....
....

Daily affirmations, I am :

....
....
....

Additional notes

....
....
....
....
....

Weight : ....

Hours Fasted : ....

My Fasting Log

Date: ....

12.00 AM	
1.00 AM	
2.00 AM	
3.00 AM	
4.00 AM	
5.00 AM	
6.00 AM	
7.00 AM	
8.00 AM	
9.00 AM	
10.00 AM	
11.00 AM	
12.00 PM	
1.00 PM	
2.00 PM	
3.00 PM	
4.00 PM	
5.00 PM	
6.00 PM	
7.00 PM	
8.00 PM	
9.00 PM	
10.00 PM	
11.00 PM	
12.00 AM	

Quality .... Sleep .... Hrs

....

....

Activity / Physical State

....

....

....

....

Mental & Emotional State

....

....

....

....

Water Intake

How could you improve today?

....

....

Daily affirmations, I am :

....

....

....

Weight : ....

Additional notes

....

....

....

....

....

....

Hours Fasted : ....

My Fasting Log

Date:

12.00 AM
1.00 AM
2.00 AM
3.00 AM
4.00 AM
5.00 AM
6.00 AM
7.00 AM
8.00 AM
9.00 AM
10.00 AM
11.00 AM
12.00 PM
1.00 PM
2.00 PM
3.00 PM
4.00 PM
5.00 PM
6.00 PM
7.00 PM
8.00 PM
9.00 PM
10.00 PM
11.00 PM
12.00 AM

Quality .... Sleep .... Hrs

Activity / Physical State

Mental & Emotional State

Water Intake

How could you improve today?

Daily affirmations, I am :

Weight : ....

Additional notes

Hours Fasted : ....

My Fasting Log

Date: ....

12.00 AM	
1.00 AM	
2.00 AM	
3.00 AM	
4.00 AM	
5.00 AM	
6.00 AM	
7.00 AM	
8.00 AM	
9.00 AM	
10.00 AM	
11.00 AM	
12.00 PM	
1.00 PM	
2.00 PM	
3.00 PM	
4.00 PM	
5.00 PM	
6.00 PM	
7.00 PM	
8.00 PM	
9.00 PM	
10.00 PM	
11.00 PM	
12.00 AM	

Quality .... Sleep .... Hrs

....
....

Activity / Physical State

....
....
....
....
....

Mental & Emotional State

....
....
....
....
....

Water 🥛🥛🥛🥛🥛🥛🥛🥛 Intake

How could you improve today?

....
....

Daily affirmations, I am :

....
....
....

Weight : ....

Additional notes

....
....
....
....
....

Hours Fasted : ....

My Fasting Log

Date:

12.00 AM	
1.00 AM	
2.00 AM	
3.00 AM	
4.00 AM	
5.00 AM	
6.00 AM	
7.00 AM	
8.00 AM	
9.00 AM	
10.00 AM	
11.00 AM	
12.00 PM	
1.00 PM	
2.00 PM	
3.00 PM	
4.00 PM	
5.00 PM	
6.00 PM	
7.00 PM	
8.00 PM	
9.00 PM	
10.00 PM	
11.00 PM	
12.00 AM	

Quality .... Sleep .... Hrs

....
....

Activity / Physical State

....
....
....
....
....

Mental & Emotional State

....
....
....
....
....

Water Intake
🥛 🥛 🥛 🥛 🥛 🥛

How could you improve today?

....
....

Daily affirmations, I am :

....
....
....

Additional notes

....
....
....
....
....

Weight : ....

Hours Fasted : ....

My Fasting Log

Date:

12.00 AM	
1.00 AM	
2.00 AM	
3.00 AM	
4.00 AM	
5.00 AM	
6.00 AM	
7.00 AM	
8.00 AM	
9.00 AM	
10.00 AM	
11.00 AM	
12.00 PM	
1.00 PM	
2.00 PM	
3.00 PM	
4.00 PM	
5.00 PM	
6.00 PM	
7.00 PM	
8.00 PM	
9.00 PM	
10.00 PM	
11.00 PM	
12.00 AM	

Quality .... Sleep .... Hrs

....

....

Activity / Physical State

....

....

....

....

Mental & Emotional State

....

....

....

Water 🥛🥛🥛🥛🥛🥛🥛 Intake

How could you improve today?

....

....

Daily affirmations, I am :

....

....

....

Weight : ....

Additional notes

....

....

....

....

....

Hours Fasted : ....

My Fasting Log

Date:

12.00 AM	
1.00 AM	
2.00 AM	
3.00 AM	
4.00 AM	
5.00 AM	
6.00 AM	
7.00 AM	
8.00 AM	
9.00 AM	
10.00 AM	
11.00 AM	
12.00 PM	
1.00 PM	
2.00 PM	
3.00 PM	
4.00 PM	
5.00 PM	
6.00 PM	
7.00 PM	
8.00 PM	
9.00 PM	
10.00 PM	
11.00 PM	
12.00 AM	

Quality .... Sleep .... Hrs
....
....

Activity / Physical State
....
....
....
....
....

Mental & Emotional State
....
....
....
....
....

Water Intake
☐ ☐ ☐ ☐ ☐ ☐ ☐ ☐

How could you improve today?
....

Daily affirmations, I am :
....
....
....

Additional notes
....
....
....
....
....

Weight : ....

Hours Fasted : ....

My Fasting Log

Date:

12.00 AM
1.00 AM
2.00 AM
3.00 AM
4.00 AM
5.00 AM
6.00 AM
7.00 AM
8.00 AM
9.00 AM
10.00 AM
11.00 AM
12.00 PM
1.00 PM
2.00 PM
3.00 PM
4.00 PM
5.00 PM
6.00 PM
7.00 PM
8.00 PM
9.00 PM
10.00 PM
11.00 PM
12.00 AM

Quality .... Sleep .... Hrs

Activity / Physical State

Mental & Emotional State

Water Intake

How could you improve today?

Daily affirmations, I am :

Additional notes

Weight : ....

Hours Fasted : ....

MAKING ~~MISTAKES~~ is part of the PROCESS

My Recipe

Name

Ingredients

Information

CALORIES:
CARBS:
PROTEIN:
FAT:
SUGAR:
OTHERS:

~ Method ~

Additional Notes

My Recipe

Name

Ingredients

Information

CALORIES:
CARBS:
PROTEIN:
FAT:
SUGAR:
OTHERS:

~ Method ~

Additional Notes

My Recipe

Name

Ingredients

Information

CALORIES:
CARBS:
PROTEIN:
FAT:
SUGAR:
OTHERS:

~ Method ~

Additional Notes

My Recipe

Name

Ingredients

Information

CALORIES:
CARBS:
PROTEIN:
FAT:
SUGAR:
OTHERS:

~ Method ~

Additional Notes

My Recipe

Name:

Ingredients

Information

CALORIES:
CARBS:
PROTEIN:
FAT:
SUGAR:
OTHERS:

~ Method ~

Additional Notes

CURRENT MEDICATION & SUPPLEMENTS

Type	Quantity	Frequency

TREATMENT RECORD

Date	Type	Notes

also by
The Gentle Notebook
LOS ANGELES

READY TO TAKE JOURNALING TO NEW LEVELS?

CHECK OUT OUR CURSE WORD EDITION!

～ Now Available ～

~ Check out our Instagram @gentlenotebook for more details ~

FOR ANY INQUIRIES OR QUESTIONS REGARDING OUR PRODUCTS, PLEASE CONTACT US AT
thegentlenotebook@gmail.com

Made in the USA
Monee, IL
28 January 2020